DEALING WITH CLAIR

MARTIN CRIMP

Martin Crimp was born in London in 1956. Since leaving
Cambridge University, where he acted and first began writing for
the stage, he has formed close links with the Orange Tree Theatre,
Richmond, which has given the first productions of *Living Remains*
(1982), *Four Attempted Acts* (1984), *A Variety of Death-Defying Acts*
(1985), and *Definitely the Bahamas* (1987) – a highly acclaimed
triple-bill directed by Alec McCowen.

His work for radio includes the Giles Cooper Award winning *Three
Attempted Acts* (1985), and the original version of *Definitely the
Bahamas*, winner of the 1986 Radio Times Drama Award.

He is currently Resident Writer at the Orange Tree under the
Thames Television resident playwright scheme.

by the same author

Three Attempted Acts
(in *Best Radio Plays of 1985*)

MARTIN CRIMP

DEALING WITH
CLAIR

NICK HERN BOOKS

A division of Walker Books Limited

A Nick Hern Book

Dealing with Clair first published in 1988 as an original paperback by
Nick Hern Books, a division of Walker Books Limited,
87 Vauxhall Walk, London SE11 5HJ

Dealing with Clair copyright © 1988 by Martin Crimp
Front cover illustration:
Study for the World's Body by R. B. Kitaj
reproduced by courtesy of Marlborough Fine Art (London) Ltd.

Set in ITC New Baskerville and printed in Great Britain by
Expression Printers Ltd, London N7 9DP

British Library Cataloguing in Publication Data
Crimp, Martin
  Dealing With Clair.
  I. Title
  822'914
ISBN 1-85459-075-8

Characters

JAMES, 50s, a cash-buyer.
MIKE, 30 ⎱
LIZ, 30 ⎰ the vendors.
CLAIR, 25, negotiator to the vendors.
ANNA, 17, the vendors' Italian nanny.
ASHLEY, 25, a tradesman.
VITTORIO, 22, a friend of ANNA.
TOBY, 25, a colleague of CLAIR.

Set

The place is London, the time the present, the month August –
with the exception of the final scene which takes place in October
of the same year.
There are 3 locations:
(1) A room in the vendors' house. Doorways to hall and kitchen.
   A tall sash window faces north.
(2) CLAIR's flat. A small 'studio' room.
(3) The vendors' garden.

Note

The much overworked indications 'pause' 'slight pause' etc. have
been replaced throughout by a single comma on a separate line.
The exact duration of any hiatus must be determined from the
context.

Dealing with Clair was commissioned by Michael Codron and first presented by arrangement with him at the Orange Tree Theatre, Richmond.

Preview: 13 October 1988. Press night: 14 October 1988.

The cast was as follows:

JAMES	Tom Courtenay
MIKE	John Michie
LIZ	Julia Hills
CLAIR	Janine Wood
ANNA	Anna Mazzotti
ASHLEY, VITTORIO and TOBY	Matthew Sim

Director: Sam Walters
Designer: Anne Gruenberg

ACT ONE

1

A room in the vendors' house. Morning. CLAIR *stands at the window, back turned.* MIKE *stands on the other side of the room, looking at her. She senses his look and turns. Both smile.*

MIKE. Look, I'm sorry, I haven't shown you the garden.

CLAIR. I don't think I need to go out there.

MIKE. I'm afraid it faces north.

CLAIR. Yes, but it's a garden. (*Both faint laugh.*) The plant along the wall –

MIKE. Yes, that's a vine.

CLAIR. Right, that's good. Vines are a good feature.

MIKE. Yes, that's why we put it in I'm afraid. Because we liked it as it was, but we've tried to do as much as we can out there with an eye to selling.

CLAIR. The slabs.

MIKE. Yes, I put down those slabs.

I'm afraid it's never had any fruit.

CLAIR. Well . . . (*Irrelevant.*)

MIKE. I'm not sure what we'd do with it if it did. We're not gardeners, are you?

CLAIR. You're joking. (*Both faint laugh.*) May I ask how long you've been here?

MIKE. It's a couple of years now. Well that's what we planned. I think any longer than that in one place and unfortunately you just start to tread water.

CLAIR. Well, in the present climate . . .

MIKE. That's right.

So.

CLAIR. Well I think we're probably looking at about a hundred and seventy-five.

MIKE. A hundred and seventy-five.

CLAIR. I think we could try it.

MIKE. Right.

CLAIR. You're not happy with that.

MIKE. We'd actually like to try a hundred and ninety.

CLAIR. A hundred and ninety.

MIKE. Well I think so, don't you.

CLAIR. You know number five went recently.

MIKE. And that was how much?

CLAIR. One seventy.

MIKE. One seventy, when was that?

CLAIR. It's a month or so now. Of course people are achieving some very good prices with these older properties. And this is a good road.

MIKE. Of course a lot of it was tenants.

CLAIR. Yes, but that's changing.

MIKE. Mind you it's quite disgusting what's happening to the tenants.

You know we've got four bedrooms here.

CLAIR. Well yes, you've got a –

MIKE. That's right, because most of these properties only have three. Number five only has three.

CLAIR. It doesn't have a window, does it.

MIKE. It doesn't have a window as such, but it's a good size. We've put our Italian girl in there actually. She loves the atmosphere. I mean here. In England. She's from Naples.

CLAIR. But not the room.

MIKE. I'm sorry?

,

No, she's very pleased with the room. It's the first time she's had her own room.

,

CLAIR. A hundred and ninety.

MIKE. Well I think we could give it a try, don't you?

CLAIR. It's pushing it.

MIKE (*faint laugh*). Well I know.

CLAIR. But of course people are getting away with it.

MIKE. Well I know. That's the thing. People are – unfortunately – getting away with it, as you say. And so, well, you see our dilemma. I mean I know the whole thing's hateful.

CLAIR. Well . . .

MIKE. But look what I mean is, is assuming we can get it, assuming we can get this price, because actually I think it's a perfectly realistic price, but assuming we can achieve that, well obviously we'd like to behave honourably in this if you see what I mean.

CLAIR. I'm sorry, how's that?

MIKE. Well what I mean is, is I simply mean I think strictly first come first served don't you, as far as any offers are concerned.

CLAIR. Well yes, if that's how you feel.

MIKE. Well don't you think that's right.

CLAIR. Well yes, of course, if that's how you feel, yes. Of course what we'd normally do is advise you to accept the best offer we receive, I mean with regard not just to the price, but taking into account who's in the best position to exchange.

MIKE. Yes. Well actually that's just the kind of thing I mean.

CLAIR. Because naturally we try to do what's best for our clients.

MIKE. Well yes. I see that.

,

CLAIR. But of course it's absolutely up to you.

MIKE. Right.

,

CLAIR. I mean if someone comes along with cash.

MIKE. Right.

CLAIR. That's all I mean.

,

Well we'll get out the details as soon as we can, Mr Walsum.

MIKE. Mike, it's Mike.

CLAIR. Mike. Fine. (*She's about to go.*)

MIKE. You don't live near the Green, do you Clair?

CLAIR. I'm sorry?

MIKE. I'm sorry, it is Clair isn't it.

CLAIR. Yes.

MIKE. I say: you don't live near –

CLAIR. No. I'm further north.

MIKE. It's only a girl crossed the road in front of my car down there. At the lights. I'm sure it was you.

CLAIR (*faint laugh*). I must look like somebody else.

MIKE. Surely not. (*That this is intended as a compliment is not lost on CLAIR. LIZ is standing in the hall doorway.*) Right Clair. (*They shake hands.*)

LIZ. So everything's alright is it?

MIKE. Fine, it's fine.

LIZ. He has told you how we feel, hasn't he?

MIKE. Yes, yes it's fine. What, is she asleep?

LIZ. Just gone.

CLAIR. She's lovely.

LIZ. She's lovely when she's asleep. No, it's just that we want to behave honourably in this.

CLAIR. Mr Walsum's told me your position.

LIZ. Because it's a hateful business.

CLAIR. No, of course, it's absolutely up to you.

LIZ. Has she seen the garden?

CLAIR. I've seen it from the window.

LIZ. I'm afraid we're not gardeners, are we.

CLAIR. Have you found somewhere?

LIZ. Actually we're going to take a flat, aren't we.

MIKE. Of course it will mean being on top of each other for a while.

LIZ. Yes it's going to be a little difficult . . .

MIKE. What with Anna . . .

LIZ. Well even without Anna, Mike. Because really it's very small. But we'll have the advantage of being cash.

CLAIR. You'll be in a good position.

LIZ. Well yes, we will. And of course we'll be less pressured.

MIKE. We want to take our time over this one.

LIZ. Because we have some friends of ours . . .

MIKE. Poppy and Max . . .

LIZ. Who panicked completely and ended up living on a railway, didn't they Mike?

They all laugh.

CLAIR. Of course, it's not necessarily a bad investment.

MIKE. Yes, but they're horribly overlooked, aren't they.

CLAIR. Listen, will you want to leave a key with us?

LIZ. Well I think we should, don't you.

MIKE. I can drop one round.

LIZ (*laughs*). Just make sure no one sees the stain.

MIKE (*laughs*). That's right. Steer them clear of the stain.

CLAIR. I'm sorry, what is that?

LIZ. I think you're standing on it actually.

CLAIR *faint laugh, looks down, moves a little.*

CLAIR. Right, I'll . . . I'll try to avoid it. We'll get the details out as soon as we can.

MIKE *and* CLAIR *go off. A baby's crying.*

LIZ. Anna. (*Louder.*) Anna, she's awake. (*She goes to the hall door and calls.*) Anna, she's awake.

She's about to go out, when the crying stops. MIKE *returns.*

MIKE. What is it?

LIZ. She's awake.

MIKE. Won't Anna go?

LIZ. She just has.

They embrace.

So she's agreed on one ninety.

MIKE. She didn't want to. She knew about number five.

LIZ. But it's only got three bedrooms.

MIKE. I told her that.

Sweet, isn't she.

LIZ. What?

MIKE. Clair.

LIZ. Is she? (*She moves away.*) Look, I'd better go.

MIKE. Hasn't Anna gone?

LIZ. It's her day off.

MIKE. She doesn't mind. Look, d'you want a coffee?

LIZ *has gone.* MIKE *goes into the kitchen. A moment passes and* ANNA *appears in a dressing-gown. She looks dejected. She sits by the telephone.* MIKE *emerges.*

Good morning.

ANNA. Is all right if I telephone, Mr Walsum.

MIKE. Provided it's not Australia. (*Faint laugh.*)

ANNA. Sorry?

MIKE. I say: as long as it's not Australia.

ANNA. No no. Italy.

MIKE. Fine, that's fine.

ANNA. You don't mind?

MIKE. No no, that's fine. Just keep it short please.

He doesn't move.

ANNA. My family.

MIKE (*going back to kitchen*). No no, that's fine. Go ahead. Just keep it short, that's all.

ANNA dials. She waits, then hangs up, stares out, is about to get up. MIKE returns with coffee.

Well you were quick.

ANNA. Is no one there.

MIKE. What in the whole of Italy? (*Laughs.*)

ANNA. I'm sorry?

MIKE. Look, has someone, well I mean you actually, you haven't, you haven't been smoking upstairs have you? It's just Mrs Walsum – Liz – Liz thought she could smell smoke up there, that's all, the other day I think it was.

ANNA. I don't smoke, Mr Walsum.

MIKE. Well no no, I know you don't. Well that's fine then, naturally.

ANNA. If I may try later on.

MIKE. By all means.

Look, we've been wondering if we've, well if we've been giving you enough spending money. Because, well, it isn't really very much.

ANNA. No no. It's fine.

MIKE. You're managing.

ANNA. It's fine.

MIKE. Because, well as you probably know, what with moving, and renting the flat, things are going to get a little tight. And I mean I don't want you to think we're the sort of people who like to . . . (*Vague gesture.*) well exploit this kind of situation. Because I know some people do with, well particularly with foreign girls they tend to take advantage.

ANNA smiles without interest.

Because you know we're not like that.

Listen, can I get you a coffee or anything?

ANNA. No thank you, Mr Walsum.

MIKE. Fine. Well. Anyway, you know where it is.

MIKE *lingers a moment more, then starts to go. At the last moment he turns.*

Look. I was just thinking, perhaps you ought to get dressed. It's just that people – hopefully – people – will be coming round to view.

ANNA (*not offended*). OK.

MIKE. I mean you know we don't mind on your day off. It's just that, well you just can't tell what's going to put people off unfortunately.

ANNA. OK.

MIKE. Not that you would, obviously, put people off. I mean you wouldn't put *me* off. But just in case somebody should come, please.

ANNA. OK, that's OK.

MIKE. Thanks, Anna.

MIKE *starts to go. At the last moment he stops as before and looks at* ANNA. *She senses his look and turns.*

Thanks.

He goes.

Blackout.

2

Evening. MIKE *and* LIZ.

LIZ. No objections to doing what?

MIKE. To leaving it on.

LIZ. But you told her we'd accept and were prepared to wait.

MIKE. Yes yes I said we accept but Clair's feeling is in case for whatever reason – because of course people do – they happen to drop out, or I don't know find it difficult to exchange, there's no harm in leaving it on. And besides I felt she was implying –

LIZ. Because I thought we'd both talked to her about this.

MIKE. Well of course, but I felt she was implying that if we got more interest we could, there would be the possibility that we could maybe push them up.

LIZ. You told her we weren't prepared to do that.

MIKE. Well she already knows we wouldn't do that.

,

LIZ. How far up?

MIKE. What?

LIZ. All I mean is –

MIKE. I don't know. She was vague.

,

Two hundred.

LIZ. As far as that.

MIKE. She seemed to think we could be looking at another five to ten thou, yes.

,

LIZ. Well that's hardly significant.

MIKE. Well no, I agree it's not particularly significant in the present climate, well five wouldn't be certainly, although perhaps ten . . . But the point is, and this is surely what we're talking about, is if it goes under offer like this in less than forty-eight hours, then maybe we're simply not asking enough.

LIZ. This is what Clair said.

MIKE. Well it's not what she *said*, no.

,

But here we are, we're paying them x per cent, and how much work will they actually have done?

,

It's complicated you see by the fact that these people, the Harraps, are in Shropshire.

LIZ. You mean they might not be genuine.

MIKE. Genuine or whatever, I just mean there's a question mark over their ability to sell. Because, as Clair said, if they're stuck up there in Wales . . .

CLAIR. England.

MIKE. England.

'

Is it?

LIZ. I think it is.

MIKE. Well wherever it is.

LIZ. Shrewsbury.

MIKE. Well wherever it is there's not much of a market.

LIZ. Just sheep.

MIKE. That sort of thing.

MIKE *lies with his head on* LIZ*'s lap.*

They've got several acres up there according to Clair. A stream. Fishing rights. You drive up through a pine forest.

LIZ. It's rural.

MIKE. That's right.

'

I mean it's not something I'd personally go along with, but surely if they had any sense they'd build on the land.

LIZ. It must be protected.

MIKE (*faint laugh*). Clair says she's got a crumbly spine.

LIZ. A what?

MIKE. Mrs Harrap. They're moving on account of her spine.

LIZ. What, are they old?

MIKE. No, they're like us apparently.

'

LIZ. And they don't mind the garden?

MIKE. Apparently they've fallen in love with the garden. They were very taken by the vine.

LIZ. So you've had a long chat with Clair.

'

MIKE. What's that supposed to mean?

LIZ. But you made it clear we're prepared to wait.

MIKE. Listen, Clair knows exactly what we've said to her and I'm sure she respects our position.

LIZ. Meaning.

MIKE. What d'you mean, meaning?

LIZ. Well meaning what?

MIKE. What do I mean by meaning?

LIZ. What do you mean by position, respects our position?

MIKE. Well exactly what I say.

LIZ. Which is?

MIKE. What?

LIZ. Well what exactly *are* you saying . . . ?

MIKE. Because if I have to explain myself every time I speak . . .

LIZ. Because it seems to me, and of course maybe I'm wrong, but it seems to me you're saying you're deferring to Clair.

MIKE. I've no intention of deferring to Clair. Come on, come on. It's simply that since we find ourselves dealing with her, then perhaps – well no, not perhaps – I think we *should* I really think we should show at least some respect for her judgement and integrity.

LIZ. Her what? (*Faint laugh.*)

So you're deferring to Clair.

MIKE. Look, I'm not deferring to Clair. She's deferring to us.

LIZ (*amused*). D'you think she always wears that skirt?

MIKE. What?

LIZ. Well she looks like a waitress.

Both faint laugh.

Blackout.

3

Morning. CLAIR *stands at the window, back turned.* JAMES *stands on the other side of the room, looking at her. She senses his look and turns. Both smile.*

JAMES. There's a good atmosphere here, isn't there. Very calm and quiet. I think that's very valuable, don't you. Because while I could never imagine living outside of a city, still I like a home to be a kind of sanctuary. Do you know it's rather like when you drive off the road, isn't it. Because you know how it is when you drive off the road onto one of those gravel tracks that leads into a mountain forest. The Pyrenees for example, the French Pyrenees. You drive slowly between the trees, then a little way in you turn off the engine. Then it strikes you. The silence.

Do you suppose it's the light? Perhaps it's the quality of the light here. That window faces north, doesn't it?

CLAIR. Yes, I think so.

JAMES. Because quite frankly I'm much happier with reflected light. Whenever I have to go a long way south I'm afraid I tend to languish rather. If I don't have a marble floor I can get very irritable. (*With equal charm:*) You do realise that sill is rotten, don't you. I could get my finger in up to the knuckle.

Both faint laugh.

JAMES (*with attack*). Bedroom four.

CLAIR. Yes?

JAMES. Have I missed bedroom four?

CLAIR. It's the room with the pictures.

JAMES. What those views of Naples?

CLAIR. Are they?

JAMES. Well aren't they? It doesn't have a window, does it. Is that why it smells of smoke?

CLAIR. It's actually quite a good size.

JAMES. Well do you know I thought it was a cupboard. I thought, well that's odd, I've stumbled into a cupboard with views of Naples. (*Faint laugh.*)

CLAIR. What's the position with your own property?

JAMES. Position in what sense?

CLAIR. I mean is your own house sold?

JAMES. I think we're at cross purposes. No, I'm not selling any houses. I think that's a hateful business, selling houses. No, I simply wish to acquire a new one here in London. Because do you know I suddenly felt terribly lost at Heathrow the other day. I drove to a hotel, but my heart wasn't in it. That's when I thought, I need something of my own here after all these years. I'm fed up with hotels, Clair, and so is my family. We're fed up with hotels here in London. I think that's a desolate kind of life, don't you.

CLAIR. You travel on business.

JAMES. I travel a lot on business.

CLAIR. So you're in a good position.

JAMES. Well I think I am, don't you?

Both faint laugh.

JAMES. The thing is, is it's an elegant house. Parts of it have obviously been abused, but underneath there is an elegant house.

CLAIR. Anything in this road is a good investment.

JAMES. Well I'm sure it is, but frankly that's not what concerns me.

You say in fact it's sold.

CLAIR. The vendors have accepted an offer.

JAMES. The vendors have accepted an offer.

CLAIR. Yes, but if someone matches it with cash.

JAMES. And what is the offer?

CLAIR. The asking price.

JAMES. Which is? I'm sorry, I . . .

CLAIR. A hundred and ninety.

JAMES. And who wishes to purchase?

CLAIR. The Harraps.

JAMES. Do I know them?

CLAIR. I'm sorry?

JAMES. Who are the Harraps?

CLAIR. Well, well they're just –

JAMES. They're just people you mean.

CLAIR. Well they're in Shropshire.

JAMES. Whereabouts is that?

CLAIR. Isn't it Wales?

JAMES. I mean whereabouts in Shropshire. Because I know Shropshire. I used to know Shrewsbury well.

CLAIR. Would you like to see the garden?

JAMES. You know, I don't think there's any need, do you? Because I like what I've seen very much, Clair.

CLAIR. I'm afraid it faces north, but there's a vine.

JAMES. We're not gardeners.

Both faint laugh. Silence.

JAMES (*with a laugh*). There's a certain kind of man who would exploit this kind of situation, isn't there Clair.

CLAIR. I'm sorry?

JAMES. I'm sorry, it is Clair, isn't it.

CLAIR. Yes.

JAMES. Well I say there's a certain kind of man who would exploit this kind of situation. I mean if I were to make an offer –

CLAIR. We'd put it to the vendors.

JAMES. You'd put it to the vendors.

CLAIR. Well naturally.

JAMES. Because I should stress I like what I've seen very much.

CLAIR. Well I'm sure they'd consider it.

JAMES. I really think I ought to meet them, don't you? We ought to talk. Because naturally I want to behave honourably in this, Clair.

CLAIR. I'll speak to the Walsums.

JAMES. Are they Dutch?

CLAIR. I don't think so.

JAMES. Because Walsum is Dutch.

CLAIR *moves away to check everything is undisturbed prior to leaving.*

JAMES. Do you know I saw a girl like you when I was on my way here.

CLAIR. Did you? (*Faint laugh.*)

JAMES (*laughs*). I'm sorry, I'm embarrassing you.

CLAIR *laughs.*

JAMES. Or perhaps it *was* you. Was it you?

CLAIR. I don't know.

'

Look, I'll try and fix up an appointment.

JAMES. Would you. Listen, I'm sorry about that.

CLAIR. It's alright.

JAMES. I mean when I called you a girl. Because it's one of those words, isn't it, it's one of those dreadful words men use to belittle women. It's funny isn't it, how you are terribly aware of everybody else's faults, and then you find you share them too. I apologise.

CLAIR. It's alright.

JAMES. Because please understand I hate that sort of thing as much as you must.

CLAIR (*as if to go*). Well look, I'll try and fix up that appointment.

JAMES. Would you. My wife will love it. The children will love that garden.

CLAIR. How many do you have?

JAMES. What did I say? Did I say children? No, just the one. (*He takes out a wallet and shows it to* CLAIR.) Marcus. A boy.

CLAIR *looks at the picture.*

JAMES. Well hardly my boy. He's my wife's boy.

'

CLAIR. She must be –

JAMES. Considerably younger. Yes, she is. But what about you, Clair. Are you married? Single? Surely not widowed? Divorced? (CLAIR *begins to laugh during this. They both laugh for a while.*) Children?

CLAIR. You're joking.

CLAIR *gives back the wallet. Silence. She fiddles with the keys.*

JAMES. I'll tell you something – and of course I may be completely wrong – but why is it I have an idea you live on a railway. Is that right?

CLAIR (*faint laugh*). Yes. Yes I do.

JAMES. I thought you did.

Isn't that odd. You see I imagine you in one of those rooms right on the railway. I see you in one of those tall old houses turned into flats, where the track passes on brick arches right outside the upper windows. If you go by at night you often have a glimpse down into these rooms. You can see people acting in a very ordinary way, as if there was no train outside. Often the light-bulbs have no shades. Isn't that odd. But then how else are they supposed to act?

CLAIR. A lot of people live on railways.

JAMES. Well of course they do. Does your bulb have a shade?

CLAIR. It's not necessarily a bad investment.

JAMES. Well of course not.

Those are the keys?

CLAIR. Yes. (*She clenches them in her fist.*) We'd better go.

JAMES. Yes, look, I'm keeping you.

CLAIR. It's just that I've got another appointment.

JAMES. Of course. (CLAIR *begins to move. He points behind her.*) The window's open.

CLAIR. Thanks.

CLAIR *goes over to the window and closes it. This takes longer than she would like.*

Right.

She crosses back to JAMES. *They go.*

Blackout.

4

Evening. MIKE *and* LIZ.

LIZ. No objections to doing what?

MIKE. To leaving it on.

LIZ. But you told her we'd accept and were prepared to wait.

MIKE. Yes yes yes, but that was before this. That was before we were talking about cash.

LIZ. So you've spoken to Clair.

MIKE. Well obviously I've spoken to Clair.

I mean Clair seems to think –

LIZ. So what's his position?

MIKE. The position is, as I understand it is, is he likes what he's seen very much and he's prepared to pay cash.

LIZ. So he's already sold. Alright, but do we *know* he's already sold?

MIKE. No no no, he's nothing to sell.

LIZ. Well it's easy enough to say that. We could say that.

MIKE. What, you don't think he's honest?

LIZ. I've not spoken to Clair.

MIKE. Well I've told you her opinion.

LIZ. Is that what she said?

MIKE. Is what what she said?

LIZ. What?

MIKE. Is what what she said?

LIZ. That in her opinion he's honest.

MIKE. Because look, it's impossible for me, please understand it's impossible for me to relate to you word for word exactly what she said.

LIZ. Word for word, no one said word for word, I just –

MIKE. Well whatever.

LIZ. I've never said word for word.

MIKE. Well whatever, Liz. Because listen, you talk to her . . .

LIZ. I'm not talking to her . . .

MIKE. Because if you talked to her you'd find out the simple fact is, is you don't go round asking if people are honest because that's not ultimately what's at issue here. What's at issue is his ability to exchange.

LIZ. Which is exactly the same thing.

MIKE. Well of course it's not.

Well listen of course it isn't. Because even if he's not 'honest' (– *gesture of inverted commas* –) whatever that actually means, meaning I suppose he's still in reality got somewhere to sell, who's to say he won't in spite of that be able to complete faster than the Harraps, who let's face it have saddled themselves with this crumbling ancestral home or spine or whatever it is surrounded by acres of land of outstanding natural beauty but no commercial value whatsoever.

,

Anyway, look, he wants to take another look round.

LIZ. When?

MIKE. Tonight. He's coming tonight.

LIZ. You could've said.

MIKE. Well he wants his wife to see it.

,

Is Anna dressed?

LIZ. Well how do I know if she's dressed?

MIKE. I would just rather she was dressed.

,

LIZ. Have you asked her about smoking?

MIKE. Because the way she wanders around here . . . No, she doesn't. She says she doesn't.

,

LIZ. I'm just worried about –

MIKE. About the Harraps. Look –

LIZ. Because we've accepted their offer.

MIKE. Yes but what does that mean? Legally it means nothing.

,

LIZ. Well legally it means nothing, but –

MIKE. You have to remember there's always been a question mark over the Harraps.

,

LIZ. I suppose they'd do it if they were in our position.

,

MIKE. In their position they'd be even more likely to. Because, alright, we may have scruples about this, but it doesn't mean that they have. Do we know them? We don't even know who they are. And it seems absurd to put ourselves under some kind of obligation to a couple of complete strangers.

,

I mean I'll be frank, I get the impression Clair finds this all rather amusing.

LIZ. You mean she's laughing at us?

,

MIKE. Well can you blame her? Because I think we're tending to blow this up into some kind of moral issue when there isn't in fact a moral issue here at all.

Doorbell. They drop their voices.

LIZ. Well we've never said it's a moral issue.

MIKE. Well that's right. (*He moves off.*)

LIZ. The stain.

MIKE. What?

LIZ. Give me time to cover the stain.

MIKE *goes.* LIZ *adjusts the rug.* MIKE *returns with* JAMES.

MIKE. And this is my wife.

JAMES. Hello.

LIZ. Hello. I'm Liz.

JAMES. I'm late. I do apologise. (*They shake hands.*)

LIZ. Well . . . Look . . .

MIKE. Please . . .

LIZ. Just go wherever you like.

JAMES. I'd quite like to take another look upstairs if I may.

LIZ. Well fine, that would be fine.

MIKE. Is Gina asleep?

LIZ. Yes, there's a baby asleep up there.

JAMES. I shan't make a sound.

LIZ. Where's Anna?

MIKE. Yes, there's our Italian girl. Well isn't she in her room.

JAMES. Well then I'll . . .

LIZ. No no. You don't need to worry. Go straight in.

MIKE (*laughs*). She's getting used to it.

JAMES. Which room is that?

LIZ. Well we think of it as the guest room, don't we Mike.

MIKE. Of course it's internally lit.

JAMES. Yes, there's no window in there, is there.

MIKE. Not a window as such, but it's actually quite a good size.

LIZ. Anna rather likes the privacy.

JAMES. Yes, but I was thinking of air.

LIZ. Oh Mike's put in an extractor, haven't you Mike. He put the
extractor in before she came.

JAMES. Well anyway I'll knock.

JAMES *goes out*. MIKE *and* LIZ *silent*.

LIZ (*sotto voce*). I thought he was bringing his wife.

MIKE (*sotto voce*). I'd better unlock the back door. (*He moves off*.)

LIZ. Mike.

MIKE. He'll want to see the garden. (*He goes*.)

LIZ *alone. Time passes. She goes over to the dark window.* JAMES *enters.*

JAMES. Isn't she lovely. How old is she?

LIZ. Seventeen.

JAMES. I mean your little girl.

LIZ (*faint laugh*). She's six months.

JAMES. Six months. Isn't that lovely. Do you know I think she has your eyes.

LIZ. Is she awake?

JAMES. I'm talking about the lids. You both have those heavy lids, don't you.

Both faint laugh.

LIZ. We were expecting your wife.

JAMES. She trusts my judgement.

LIZ. Isn't she curious?

JAMES. No. (*Both faint laugh.*) There's a good atmosphere here isn't there. It's very calm and quiet. I was saying to Clair it reminds me of driving off the road. I mean one of those gravel tracks that takes you into a forest. The sound of the crushed gravel is quite shocking. But when you finally stop between the trees and turn off the engine, it immediately strikes you. The silence. And as you walk away from the gravel you make no sound at all on the decaying needles. Do you know the Pyrenees at all, the French Pyrenees?

LIZ. What, do you travel on business?

JAMES. I travel a lot on business.

LIZ. Which is?

JAMES. Pictures. I deal in pictures.

LIZ. Oh. Is that interesting?

JAMES. Well I like it.

LIZ. Yes, we like France, but it's getting so expensive.

JAMES. I know. France is expensive. I have a little house there. It's hardly much bigger than this actually. But I've had the floors replaced and it's costing me a fortune. Most of the year I'm not even there.

LIZ. Would you like to see the garden?

JAMES. Well I don't think I need to, do you Liz. It is Liz, isn't it. Well I don't think I need to, Liz.

LIZ. I suppose it's dark.

JAMES. Well exactly. (MIKE *appears in the doorway*). There's a certain kind of man who would exploit this kind of situation, isn't there.

MIKE. Does he want to see the garden?

LIZ. I think it's too dark.

MIKE. I'm afraid it faces north.

JAMES. You do know that sill is rotten?

MIKE. No, which one is that?

JAMES. The one in here. I was saying to Clair: you could get your finger in there up to the knuckle. (*Laughs.*) She seemed quite confident that you would have it repaired.

LIZ. Well . . . (*She looks at* MIKE.)

MIKE. Well yes if –

JAMES. Well that's settled. Good.

Are you taking the carpets? I noticed something's been spilled on this one. What is it? Wine?

MIKE. Turmeric, it's turmeric.

JAMES. What's that?

LIZ. It's a spice, a colouring.

JAMES. Turmeric. So are you taking them?

MIKE. They'd be negotiable.

JAMES. Only if you are, it will save me the bother you see of ripping them out.

LIZ. The thing is, is Clair has explained our position, hasn't she.

JAMES. That's right. She says you're prepared to ditch your buyer for a cash sale.

MIKE. Well not exactly ditch . . .

JAMES. No? Well then we must be at cross purposes, because she told me you would.

LIZ. No, yes, well that's right, we probably will.

JAMES. You probably will.

LIZ. Well we almost certainly will, won't we Mike, only we still have qualms.

JAMES. Have I misunderstood?

MIKE. What Liz means is it's more a matter of how we proceed.

LIZ. That's right.

JAMES. But if you still have qualms . . .

MIKE. Yes, about how to proceed.

JAMES. Well isn't that obvious?

MIKE. Well not entirely . . .

JAMES. I mean if you simply instruct Clair . . .

LIZ. Well obviously it would be through Clair . . .

JAMES. Because I need to be clear in my own mind. You either ditch them or you don't.

MIKE. Right. (*All faint laugh.*) Well I think we will, don't you.

LIZ. The thing is, is the Harraps are in Shropshire.

MIKE. I think we'd probably feel differently, wouldn't we, if . . .

LIZ. And of course there's a problem with her spine.

MIKE. Apparently she has a crumbly spine.

JAMES. A what?

MIKE. A crumbly spine.

JAMES. A crumbly spine.

   Led by JAMES, *all three let themselves go with hearty laughter.*

JAMES (*wiping his eyes*). So they're quite old.

LIZ. No, they're like us apparently.

JAMES. Listen, I like what I've seen very much.

MIKE. Well obviously we'll –

JAMES. That's right, I think the next thing I should do is speak again to Clair. I must say I think we're very lucky to be dealing with Clair. Because I have a feeling she's honest.

MIKE. That's right. A lot of them aren't.

JAMES. A lot of them are crooks, let's face it.

LIZ. I just wish she wasn't quite so cold.

MIKE. What? Clair?

LIZ. Yes. I find her cold.

MIKE. I wouldn't've called her cold.

JAMES. She seems perfectly human.

MIKE. Well that's right. Because a lot of them aren't.

JAMES. Some of those young men. . . (MIKE *and* JAMES *laugh*.)

LIZ. I just think you could never get to know somebody like that.

JAMES. But is it really necessary to know people in that way? Because what you call cold, isn't that just a way of dealing with strangers. Because in a city you spend so much time dealing, don't you, with strangers. And I'm not sure what would be achieved by letting them all see into your heart. Personally I find that kind of intimacy rather stifling. No, I'd much rather feel I can walk right past someone I've known for years without the least obligation to acknowledge them. I like to know that our clothes can touch for a moment on the crowded pavement, but our eyes, even if they meet, which is unlikely, our eyes agree to say nothing. And why should we speak? (*He makes to go*.) No, I wouldn't've called her cold.

LIZ. So you'll talk to Clair.

JAMES. I'll talk to her in the morning.

MIKE. She has put you in the picture about the price.

JAMES. Yes, a hundred and ninety, is that right?

MIKE. Yes, as a rough guide.

JAMES. I'm sorry?

MIKE. Well Clair's probably told you that we're, well looking for a slightly better figure.

JAMES. No, she didn't mention that.

MIKE. Because . . .

LIZ. Because Clair feels, I think she feels we've been a bit, well cautious with the price quite frankly.

JAMES. Cautious.

LIZ. Yes.

JAMES. No. No she didn't tell me that.

'

Well look, I'll talk to her in the morning.

MIKE (*faint laugh*). It's a hateful business, isn't it.

JAMES. I know, I know. Goodbye.

LIZ. Goodnight.

MIKE shows JAMES out. A baby is crying.

LIZ. Anna. (*Louder.*) Anna, she's awake. Anna, Gina's awake.

A moment passes. The crying stops. MIKE returns.

MIKE. What is it?

LIZ. She's awake.

MIKE. Anna will go.

LIZ. Poor Anna.

Both laugh. They embrace.

What do you think?

MIKE. Well what do you think?

LIZ. Well obviously he's genuine.

MIKE. Yes.

LIZ. But he was surprised about the price.

MIKE. No, he was bluffing.

LIZ. Yes, I thought he was bluffing.

'

He deals in pictures.

MIKE. What, you had a chat?

LIZ. I actually think he's rather charming.

MIKE. What?

LIZ. Mr James.

MIKE. Is he? (*He moves away.*)

What sort of pictures?

LIZ (*faint laugh*). I've no idea.

Blackout.

5

Morning. ASHLEY *in white overalls, back turned, is examining the ceiling.* ANNA *appears in the hall doorway and stops. Throughout this scene* ASHLEY *shows no sexual interest in* ANNA.

ANNA. Sorry.

ASHLEY. No, it's OK. You can come through.

ANNA. I want to go to the kitchen.

ASHLEY. Sure. Go ahead.

ANNA *goes out.* ASHLEY *spreads a dust-sheet. She returns.*

ASHLEY. Italian?

ANNA. I'm sorry?

ASHLEY. You Italian?

ANNA. Yes.

ASHLEY. That's right you've got those eyes. You see my wife's Italian – well half Italian – she's got those eyes. So whereabouts you from?

ANNA. Naples.

ASHLEY. Yea that's nice. Naples is nice. Her mother's from Turin – you know – Fiat. You know Turin at all?

ANNA. Yes, a little.

ASHLEY. Torino, yea?

Both faint laugh. ASHLEY *takes out a wallet.*

Look, that's Anna.

ANNA. Anna.

ASHLEY. That's right. Anna's my wife. Then that's Lisa, Timothy and Rachel. Three, eighteen months, two months. Handful, yea. (*Giving the wallet to* ANNA *who's not very interested.*) No, that's alright, have a look. (*He moves away, leaving* ANNA *with the pictures, and spreads another sheet.*) Handful, yea. (*She gives back the wallet.*) So, what, you studying are you?

ANNA. I'm the nanny.

ASHLEY. The nanny. Right.

So how many've they got then?

ANNA. One.

ASHLEY. One.

ANNA. It's a girl.

ASHLEY. Well then you're laughing aren't you.

ANNA. Sorry?

ASHLEY. Just one, you're laughing.

So, what, she goes out to work does she?

ANNA. Mmm?

ASHLEY. Mrs Walsum. Goes out to work.

ANNA. Oh no.

ASHLEY. No.

Right.

ANNA. She's very busy though.

ASHLEY. Right.

Anna, my wife, she'd like to, you know, she'd like to go back to work.

ANNA. Yes?

ASHLEY (*faint laugh*). So how old is she?

ANNA. I don't know. Twenty-nine . . . maybe thirty.

ASHLEY. I mean the kid.

ANNA. The kid, she's six months.

ASHLEY. Six months, well then she sleeps a lot, yea? I mean I think they do, particularly girls.

ANNA. I think particularly boys sleep a lot.

ASHLEY. Yea? Yea you may be right.

ANNA. And you know she wakes up at six thirty in the morning.

ASHLEY. Yea? Six thirty, that's when I leave the house.

ANNA *about to go.*

ASHLEY. Come here come here, I want to show you something. No it's alright, I just want to show you something. Look. No no, look at this. (*He indicates the ceiling.*) Because what your governor wants me to do, alright, is hack out that sill, because he's right, it's rotten. But if I was him *that's* what would worry me. Because what you're looking at up there is a fractured cornice, and for my money it means the joists of this floor we're standing on are decaying, you with me?

'

Because of course this is a very nice road. It's very quiet. You're near the green. There's a nice atmosphere. New cars. Trees. But I've been in one or two of these houses, and once you get the boards up . . . (*Laughs, shakes his head.*) I mean what we're talking about here is serious timber decay, we're talking about the structure, you with me?

ANNA. The structure.

ASHLEY. That's right.

'

I mean I live on a railway myself, but it's what I call a proper house. The sills've got throats. You know what I mean by a throat? A throat, it's a groove runs under the sill. It clears the water. These sills, they've got no throats. The water can't get away.

LIZ *appears in the hall doorway.*

ASHLEY. Of course the kids love the trains. Well it's stimulation for them, isn't it.

LIZ. There won't be a lot of dust, will there?

ASHLEY. Shouldn't be.

LIZ. It's just we have a baby.

ASHLEY. Shouldn't be, love.

LIZ. Fine, that's fine. Anna, do you think you could go and get dressed now. (ANNA *goes.*) It's quite impossible to get that girl dressed before eleven o'clock. (*Faint laugh.*)

ASHLEY. Anna?

LIZ. Yes, she's Italian.

ASHLEY. Yea, my wife's Italian.

LIZ. Is she?

ASHLEY. Well half Italian –

LIZ. Look, I have to go out so I'd better give you this now. (*She gives him a cheque folded in half.*) Yes, look I'm sorry, I've only just realised I don't have the cash. You don't mind a cheque, do you.

Because obviously you'd rather have the cash obviously, but somehow this morning things have . . . Well I'm sure you must have mornings like that.

ASHLEY. It's just that we did say –

LIZ. Look, I know. Well if you'd rather wait.

ASHLEY. No no. It's fine.

ANNA. Because look, if you're prepared to wait.

ASHLEY. It's not a problem.

LIZ. Look, I feel awful about this.

ASHLEY. No. Please. It's not a problem.

LIZ. It is right, isn't it.

ASHLEY. Sure it is, yea. (*He pockets the cheque without looking at it.*)

LIZ. Well if there's any problem.

ASHLEY. Right.

LIZ *makes to go, turns back.*

LIZ. Will there be a lot of noise?

ASHLEY. Shouldn't be.

LIZ. Only she's asleep.

ASHLEY. Well if you could find me something . . .

LIZ. How's that? Well of course, yes, what is it?

ASHLEY. I mean if you could find me something like a blanket I could wrap it round my hammer.

LIZ *forces a smile.*

Blackout.

6

Morning. The room is empty, the phone ringing. JAMES enters from the kitchen and stands looking at the phone. A moment passes. CLAIR enters rapidly from the hall. As she does so, the ringing stops.

JAMES (*with enthusiasm*). It's beginning to feel like home, isn't it. Don't you think that's a good sign?

CLAIR. Mr Walsum's had the sill repaired.

JAMES. I know he has. Wasn't that prompt of him. Can I get you lunch?

CLAIR. I'm sorry?

JAMES. I wondered if after this you would like lunch somewhere.

CLAIR. I've got sandwiches.

JAMES. Sandwiches.

CLAIR. Yes, I've got sandwiches in the office.

JAMES. Well, another time.

CLAIR. The Walsums are very pleased with your offer.

JAMES. Well naturally I'm very pleased they've accepted. Because it's important who you buy from and I think they're rather nice people, don't you Clair.

CLAIR *smiles.*

JAMES. No, you're quite right, they're not at all are they. Not like us for example. Because we *are*, aren't we, we *are* nice people. Well aren't we nice people?

CLAIR *smiles*.

JAMES. No, you're quite right, we're not at all.

CLAIR. Speak for yourself.

JAMES. What? (*Brief laugh.*)

,

Look, I'm sorry to have dragged you back.

CLAIR. Yes, I wasn't quite clear –

JAMES. I just want to be sure.

,

Two hundred thousand pounds. (*Confidentially:*) Do you think it's worth it Clair? Am I being made a fool of?

CLAIR. I'm not buying it.

JAMES. Yes, but do you?

CLAIR. Yes I do.

JAMES. Well I'm glad you said that. I'm glad you said that, Clair. Because so do I. And after all, what's money?

CLAIR *smiles*.

JAMES. Well. Yes.

,

CLAIR. This road will always be desirable.

JAMES. Listen: a train stops right outside your window. The passengers' faces are all pressed against the glass. Doesn't that worry you?

CLAIR. You get used to trains. You don't think about them.

JAMES. What are they anyway, are they egg? Your sandwiches. Are they egg?

CLAIR. No.

JAMES. I'll tell you something. And of course I may be completely wrong. But I'm pretty certain you have one of those beds, don't you, that folds up into a sofa. Is that right? Look, I'm sorry, I'm not embarrassing you am I? All I mean is, is it begins as a sofa. You spend the evening sitting on it, most probably on your own.

Then at a certain time, and although the time is utterly up to you, it's probably always the same time near enough, you get off the sofa, and you unfold it and rearrange it in a special way which once seemed rather complicated but now comes to you as second nature, and you get ready for bed and you get into it. Please stop me if I'm wrong. And in the morning you are woken by the alarm – if not by the trains – and you get up, and you get ready for work. But before you go out, you turn the bed back into a sofa again. Except on those days – and this is the nub – except on those days when you're late for work perhaps, or you simply can't face it, you simply can't face folding the bloody thing up. So you leave it. But the moment you get home in the evening you take one look at it, you take one look at it and you regret having left it like that. Unmade like that. Bitterly. Because immediately there is a dilemma. I don't think it's too much to speak of a dilemma, do you. And the last thing any of us wants is a dilemma, particularly in the evenings. Because either you turn your bed back into a sofa, knowing that in a few hours you'll have to turn your sofa back into a bed again. Or of course you leave it. The disadvantage in this case being that desolate feeling that nothing in the room has really happened to distinguish between morning, evening, and night.

CLAIR (*not unamused*). No, I'm afraid you're completely wrong.

JAMES. Because there are times when I think it must be rather terrible to live on your own.

CLAIR. What makes you think I live on my own?

I like being on my own.

JAMES. It has its advantages.

CLAIR. It certainly does. (*Both faint laugh.*) Your wife hasn't been, has she.

JAMES. She trusts my judgement.

CLAIR. Isn't she curious?

JAMES. I'll let you into a secret: I've decided not to tell her till we exchange. A house in London, she's absolutely no idea.

CLAIR. The thing is is Mr and Mrs Walsum want to exchange within the next couple of weeks if possible.

JAMES. Yes, of course.

CLAIR. Because they did already have a firm offer.

JAMES. Which they rejected.

CLAIR. Yes, but on the understanding there'd be a speedy exchange of contracts.

JAMES. Yes.

Listen –

CLAIR. I think they'd feel happier if they'd heard from your solicitors.

JAMES. I'm instructing them this afternoon.

CLAIR. Fine, that's fine. It's simply that –

JAMES. Then I'm afraid I'm going on to Rome. A client of mine wants me to take a look at a picture. It's a complete waste of time. You can see from the slides it's not genuine. For one thing it appears to have more than one vanishing point which is a curiosity to say the least for the period in question.

CLAIR. Right, so what exactly is your position now?

JAMES. You know what I mean by vanishing point?

Listen, you seem to be asking me whether I'm honest.

CLAIR. Well of course not, it's simply that –

JAMES. Because quite frankly Clair –

CLAIR. I'm sorry, it's simply that they were beginning to panic.

JAMES. Well please set their minds at rest.

CLAIR. And I think they feel that since they've deferred to you –

JAMES. In what way have they deferred to me?

CLAIR. In that they did have a firm offer.

JAMES. Which they rejected.

CLAIR. Yes, but since they've now deferred –

JAMES. I think you'll find that I have deferred to them, Clair, in this business.

Brief sound of laughter off.

Is there somebody here?

They listen. Silence. CLAIR *moves to the hall doorway.*

CLAIR (*calls*). Hello. (*Louder.*) Hello. (*Silence.*) There shouldn't be. (*She fiddles with the keys.*)

JAMES. Perhaps it's next door. Those are flats next door, aren't they.

CLAIR. Yes, but they're owner-occupied.

JAMES. Like yours.

CLAIR (*laughs*). I couldn't afford to live here.

JAMES. But the principle is the same. They all have beds that fold into chairs. These . . . Harraps, they're eating their hearts out, are they.

CLAIR. They've been a little aggressive on the phone.

JAMES. Have they? I love it up there by the Welsh border, don't you. If only it wasn't death. Because it's very beautiful, but really it is death.

CLAIR. So we're talking about maybe a fortnight.

JAMES. At the outside, Clair.

CLAIR. Well I'll tell them.

JAMES. Listen, if I have any problems I'll give you a call, because after all I have your number.

CLAIR. Fine, that's fine.

JAMES. Not egg.

Do you know Italy at all?

CLAIR. I've been to Venice.

JAMES. Seven days was that, or a long weekend?

CLAIR. I'm sorry, I don't like being laughed at.

JAMES. Laughed at? Clair . . .

Unfortunately I have to fly. Because my real passion is for trains, particularly sleeping trains. I think a cubicle in a train is perhaps the most perfect place to sleep, don't you. There's hot water and prohibitions in several languages. The rhythm of the track lulls you asleep. You dream your way under the mountains, then when you wake up, you lift the blind and the Mediterranean is right outside the window, lapping on empty beaches. In the east the sun's coming up behind the vineyards, and the great marble cities: Pisa, Florence, Rome, Naples.

'

For some people sleeping on trains is a kind of compulsion, did you know that? Last thing at night they disappear from the end of the platform. They jump down onto the ballast and follow the electrified rails until they find an unlocked train. Of course the water in the first class washrooms has gone cold, but the benches retain some warmth from the last passengers. Yes I know it might be argued they have no other homes, but I think the truth of it is, deep in their hearts, they're in love with trains, don't you.

'

All I meant Clair, was that personally twenty-four hours in Venice is too much for me. What a foul wet place. Thank god it's sinking.

Blackout.

7

Firstly we hear CLAIR *speaking in the darkness. Then the lights come up faintly on* CLAIR's *flat at night.* CLAIR *is sitting on an unmade bed, talking softly on the phone.*

CLAIR (*ad lib*). Uh-hu. – Uh-hu. – Mmm. – Yes. – Yes. (*Faint laugh.*)

The lights come up.

No, I've just got in.

No, it's alright, I don't mind at all. – No. (*Faint laugh.*)

That's right, it's getting pretty busy at the moment. A lot of new things are coming on.

No. Fine, I'm fine. We've got a good line, haven't we. You sound very close. – I said you sound very close. – (*Faint laugh.*) That's right.

(*Without conviction:*) Well yes, of course you must.

No, you know you're welcome to stay. I just think it might be . . . You might find it difficult, that's all. – Well there isn't that much room, that's all I mean. – Well, we'll see.

Exciting? You're joking. I'm afraid I'm just sitting here. – I said I'm just sitting here.

I can't think of any. – No, I can't think of any news particularly.

(*Faint laugh.*) What?

Oh, nothing exciting. Just the usual things I wear to work. Skirt. Blouse. – No, the black one. (*Referring to her skirt.*)

The sound of a high-speed train passing in the middle-distance. The peak of the sound no more than ten seconds, just loud enough to suspend conversation. As it passes, the train projects shadows across the room.

I'm sorry?

Yes, it was a train. (*Faint laugh.*) Really, I don't think about it.

Euston, I think it's Euston.

Look, I've told you, I like being on my own. I'm much happier on my own.

Well I'm sorry but I don't agree. – I'm not angry. I just don't quite see how me having a man here would make you any happier, that's all.

People? I spend all day with people.

A train passes as before.

(*Over the noise:*) I said I spend all day with people.

Well that's right. (*Changing the subject.*) Look, did I tell you I've decorated. – Yes, I did the whole place on Bank Holiday Monday. Started at ten and worked right through to two in the morning. – (*Laughs.*) Well I was waiting for the undercoat to dry. – Of course I did it on my own.

Bed? Yes, I suppose so. I haven't actually made it yet. (*Faint laugh.*) That's right, this morning there wasn't time and . . . I don't know, I just can't face it at the moment.

Yes I know, I just think it will make it easier to sell. – Well if I don't sell now I'm just treading water.

I don't see it's particularly hateful. It's just how it is, I'm afraid.

Peach, it's mostly peach. – Yes, that's what I thought.

(*Becoming distressed:*) Please . . . Please . . .

Look, he's not my young man. Please . . .

Will you listen to me – Will you listen to me, I don't want to talk about Toby, thank you very much.

No, of course he's not here. You must be joking.

Please, it's finished. – Yes, that's what I said, it's finished.

Well I don't know how you can say you like him when you've never even seen him.

No, we've not had an argument. (*Bitter laugh.*) You couldn't argue with Toby. No, it's just some men, really I don't actually want to talk about it, it's just some men have a certain way of treating you. I don't know, it's like . . .

No no, nothing like that. Of course not.

Look, I've said, it's nothing like that. – Well of course I'm sure. No, it's just, well it sounds stupid, but it's just I went out with him after work with some other people, for a meal. – Oh I don't know, Italian. And we'd all agreed, I really don't want to talk about it actually . . . Well it's just we'd all agreed to pay for ourselves, so when the bill came I thought we could just, well obviously, divide it by seven or eight, or however many of us there were. But Toby started this business where we all had to, because we'd all had roughly the same, but he felt, and I suppose he was right in a way, felt that the two of us had probably had less than the others, so anyway of course he asked for the menu back and he started this business where we all had to add up our own separate amounts. And of course the separate totals, I don't know this sounds so ridiculous, but they didn't add up which didn't really surprise anyone to the amount on the bill. – That's right, and so we kept going over and over who'd had what to try and make them add up to the amount on the bill. And of course everyone was getting a bit irritable, and the waitress was, well you can imagine, laughing at us. But when I said to Toby, look can't we just divide the bill, please, by seven or eight or however many of us there were, he just looked at me and he carried on. He carried on. – That's right. Which is what I mean, that some men have a way of treating you, as if you don't, actually, not just an inferior, but don't actually, well, exist. I suppose. Except as . . . Because sometimes I get the idea you just have to talk to a man and it's assumed . . .

Yes. Respect. I suppose that's what I mean about Toby.

Does he? (*Faint laugh.*) Well then, you know all about it. So. Finished. End of subject, yes? Look, anyway, how is he, how is Dad?

Well he shouldn't've lifted them. – I say surely he shouldn't've been lifting them.

She lights a cigarette.

Uh-hu. – Uh-hu.

Well surely that's not part of your spine. – Is it?

No. Look. Sorry, I was dreaming. – (*Louder.*) Dreaming.

Oh, I don't know . . . I was just thinking it might be nice to get away for a while, that's all.

(*Faint laugh.*) Anywhere really.

Listen, no one's making any offers. – No. I'd go on my own again. I imagine.

(*With anger:*) Exactly what I say: I *imagine* I'd go on my own.

I know. I'm sorry. I must be tired. Did I say we've started opening in the evenings now. – That's right, it's a long day.

Listen, I don't want to change. Although maybe eventually . . . I mean I'm dealing with people, which is what I'm good at, and they're . . . they've some very interesting properties. – Properties. – Yes, and I'm actually very happy with what I do.

Well I'm sorry if I don't sound happy. I mean I've only just got in. I can't be expected to –

Well I'm not saying they're all nice. But generally . . .
I mean when things go wrong obviously we sometimes get aggression. Or whatever. Because we're caught in the middle of it. – (*Laughs.*) Aggression, mum, not violence.
– Well of course it's not the same.

OK.

Fine, yes I will.

Give him my love.

Yes I will, of course I will.

(*Faint laugh.*) No, of course I don't mind. I like you to ring. – I know. Look, I'll write you a long letter, send all the news.

OK. Yes.

Yes, give him my love.

Yes, yes I will. Goodnight then.

Yes, goodnight.

Goodnight.

CLAIR *hangs up. The sound of a train approaching. As if suddenly feeling cold she wraps her arms around herself, a gesture which is at the same time sensual but lonely. The train passes, projecting shadows across the room. She doesn't move. The light fades with the sound of the receding train.*

Interval.

ACT TWO

1

Night. ANNA *kneels downstage with cards, playing patience on the floor, beside her a glass of orange juice.* MIKE *and* LIZ *are sprawled on a sofa, drinking wine.* MIKE *is noticeably drunk.*

MIKE. I just mean, look all I mean is, well come on, I'm right.

LIZ. I don't think you are. I'm sorry.

MIKE. Well come on, you know I'm right. Because look, you're in a room, right, with a man –

LIZ (*with a laugh*). I'm sorry, you don't know. You just don't know what you're talking about.

MIKE. No come on, come on. Listen to me. You're not listening to me. I mean you know what I'm talking about, don't you Anna. (ANNA *takes no notice.* MIKE *faint laugh.*) Yea, that's right. You see Anna will bear me out on this. Because you're in a room right, with a man. Or anywhere, not just a room, anywhere. And there you are. There you are and you're talking about, well look I'm not talking about what you're talking about, because that's not my point – I mean come on come on if you won't listen . . . Because the point is, and look this is my point, is you both know, you *both know* what's going on. But no one admits it, that's all. I mean you can say what you like –

LIZ. I didn't say a word.

MIKE. Yea, say what you like but you know – you *both know* – that I'm right because this – listen I don't see that it's funny – because this is human nature.

LIZ. It's certainly your nature.

MIKE. Alright, well that's what I'm saying.

(*He points at* ANNA*'s cards.*) Snap. (*Faint laugh.* ANNA *looks up briefly.*) I didn't know Italians played that.

LIZ. Patience?

MIKE. Yea yea. Patience.

,

What did I say? I mean take, let's take Clair for example.

LIZ (*laughs*). Clair?

MIKE. Yea yea. I mean what's so funny, I mean that's just an example isn't it. Clair. The waitress. Because, what, you know, I've spoken to Clair, what, a few times, quite a few times now, and that's exactly the sort of thing I mean. Because, you know, it's prices . . . it's properties . . . it's a serious business, but we both know what's going on, Clair and me, because that's what's always going on. And d'you see, that's all I'm saying. (MIKE *leans forward to pour wine into* ANNA*'s glass. She puts her hand over it without looking up*.) That's all I mean. Look at this, she's Italian she doesn't drink.

LIZ. You mean you want to rape Clair.

MIKE. No no no. Come on. Come *on*, will you. Because who's talking about violence? (*To* ANNA , *ignored:*) Did I say anything about violence? No I mean what is this? I mean I'm just talking about something that happens, something you know that happens, and here you are, here the two of you are, and you're trying to turn it into a moral issue.

LIZ (*amused*). Who said anything about a moral issue?

MIKE. Because what you're both trying to do is completely distort what I'm trying to say. Because – no it's not, it's not funny – because I'm not talking about violence, aggression, or whatever. Because alright, we know there's something going on, and it's sexual, but it's based on respect. Respect is all part of it. I mean what does she mean, what do you mean rape Clair. Because let's face it we're not talking about, I don't know . . . Arabs, are we. We're not talking about, you know, Italians, are we Anna, or anything like that. I mean I'm not criticising but it's different, that's a different kind of society.

ANNA. I'm going to bed.

LIZ. Goodnight.

ANNA *goes.*

MIKE. Yea, goodnight. (*Calls after* ANNA*:*) Look, no offence. (*Faint laugh.*)

MIKE *drinks.*

LIZ. You know she's been phoning Italy again.

MIKE. Mmm?

LIZ. Anna. I caught her on the phone again to Italy.

MIKE. How d'you know?

LIZ. Because she was speaking Italian. (*She drinks.*) Although of course she denied it.

MIKE. She denied she was speaking Italian.

LIZ. She denied it was Italy.

MIKE. Sometimes there's no one there, you know. The whole of Italy. No one there. Turin. Pisa. Florence. Rome. Naples . . .

LIZ (*on the word 'Rome'*). I mean why can't she *write* to her mother?

MIKE. The lights are all on but there's nobody there.

Look, she knows the position on phone calls.

LIZ lies with her head on MIKE's lap.

LIZ. Anyway she'd eat you alive.

MIKE. What?

LIZ. Clair.

MIKE. Well I wouldn't mind.

Both faint laugh.

LIZ. Let's go to bed.

MIKE. Because what's he coming back for anyway?

LIZ. He wants to measure up.

MIKE. Measure up. What does he want to measure up?

LIZ. I don't know.

MIKE. Because what did he do last time?

LIZ. Well obviously he didn't measure up.

Both find this funny.

MIKE. So this is what Clair said.

LIZ. Clair was at lunch.

MIKE. They let them out, do they, for lunch. Because he does know I suppose, he does know in two days we exchange.

LIZ. Well of course he knows.

MIKE. Well as long as he knows.

LIZ. Well of course he does. Let's go to bed.

MIKE (*amused*). You know he's never been outside, don't you.

LIZ (*amused*). What?

MIKE. Clair told me –

LIZ. In one of your conversations.

MIKE. In one of our conversations she said to me, he's never been out in the garden.

LIZ. So?

MIKE. Well you'd think he'd be curious.

LIZ. Well obviously he isn't.

Both find this funny.

MIKE. Because I think he's cold.

LIZ. Well I think he's charming.

MIKE. Anyway, you can ask him.

LIZ. Ask him if he's charming?

MIKE. If he's curious. No, you can ask him tomorrow if he's curious at all.

LIZ. I won't be here tomorrow. I've told you: I'm at the flat.

'

MIKE. You're at the flat. Right. So how's the flat.

LIZ. It's alright. It's just –

MIKE. Look, if we don't take this flat we won't be cash.

LIZ. I know, I know.

MIKE. Because if you want people to treat you like . . .

LIZ. I know.

MIKE. Shit. Or whatever. Eating your heart out. Or whatever.

'

What're you looking at?

LIZ. What's that line?

MIKE. It's a crack. Just a crack.

LIZ. It's just I think, you know, we might get on top of each other.

MIKE. Well I'm sure we might. I'm sure that's, you know, a strong possibility. (*They laugh.*) Or whatever.

LIZ. Come on, let's go upstairs.

MIKE. What's wrong?

LIZ. Anna might come in.

MIKE. Anna might come in. (*Faint laugh.*) You're right.

LIZ. Well she might.

MIKE. Yes she might. I'm sure that's, you know, a strong possibility.

LIZ. Come on. (*She gets up.*)

MIKE. I mean she knows what I'm talking about. Anna knows what I mean, don't you Anna.

LIZ takes her glass and reaches for the bottle to clear it away.

MIKE. Hey.

MIKE stops her and drains the bottle into his glass. LIZ then takes her own glass and the empty bottle out into the kitchen. MIKE stretches out, but doesn't drink, leaving his glass on the floor.

Because there you are, I mean, you both know – you *both know* – what's going on . . . Because, well that's all we're talking about isn't it . . . (*Faint laugh. Then after a moment a longer louder laugh as if something unexpectedly amusing has struck him.*)

LIZ reappears at the doorway.

LIZ. Are you coming?

She goes up to MIKE.

LIZ (*gently*). Come on, let's go to bed.

She touches him. He's asleep. LIZ remains a moment, then goes.

Blackout.

2

Morning. The cards from the previous night remain on the floor where
ANNA *left them.* CLAIR *and* JAMES *enter.*

JAMES. Well the poor man, what was he lifting?

CLAIR (*laughs*). Slabs.

JAMES. Slabs.

CLAIR. Concrete slabs. He's building a patio.

JAMES. What's that?

CLAIR. Well it's –

JAMES. Yes, I think I have an idea, Clair.

CLAIR. Please don't make fun of them.

JAMES. I'm sorry. And do they live on a railway too?

CLAIR. No.

JAMES. It's not hereditary.

CLAIR. No. (*They both laugh.*)

JAMES. I'm sorry.

I'm prying.

CLAIR. You're good at that.

JAMES. Yes I am, aren't I. (*Both laugh.*) When I rang do you know
they wanted to send somebody else. They were trying to fob me
off with one of those dreadful boys.

CLAIR. Toby.

JAMES. You're right. That was the name. He said, I'll come and
meet you with the key. I said will you please listen to me, I'm
dealing exclusively with Clair in this matter. (*Both laugh.*) What's
he like?

CLAIR. Toby? (*Shrugs.*)

JAMES. Would we've hit it off?

CLAIR. No. (*They laugh.*)

JAMES. Is he in front of you or behind you?

CLAIR. He's to the side.

JAMES. The left.

CLAIR. Yes.

JAMES. You turn to your left and there's Toby. He's on the phone but he's looking at you.

CLAIR. No, he's working.

,

JAMES. Yes, of course he is.

CLAIR. I asked him to come.

JAMES. Did you?

CLAIR. I should be at lunch.

JAMES. We can have lunch after this.

CLAIR. Because now we're having to work in the evenings . . .

JAMES. And this is work?

CLAIR. Yes. Yes, it's a long day.

,

JAMES. Yes, of course it is.

CLAIR. Sometimes it's a strain dealing with people.

JAMES. I can imagine.

CLAIR. Because we're caught in the middle of it.

JAMES. Which is what you're paid for.

CLAIR. Yes.

JAMES. Whatever per cent. And you enjoy it. .

CLAIR. Yes.

JAMES. Because you like dealing with people. You like people.

CLAIR. Yes. Yes I do.

JAMES. So why is it you don't seem happy, Clair?

CLAIR. I'm perfectly happy.

JAMES. But you don't sound happy.

CLAIR (*with anger*). Well I'm sorry.

,

JAMES. Listen, I ought to get on. (*He takes out a folding surveyor's rule.*) It will be rather unfortunate if these pieces of mine don't fit.

JAMES *measures.* CLAIR *moves away. She pokes at the cards with her shoe.*

CLAIR. Last week I did a valuation on the other side of the green. Two beds, two reception rooms. The lady, her husband had just died but he'd left her only a proportion of the house – or that's the impression I had. Because she obviously didn't want to leave – they'd lived there for thirty years – but she said it made sense to go, because of her children, and because she really needed somewhere smaller now I suppose, now she was on her own. The property required complete modernisation of course. New bathroom. New kitchen. But it had an unusually large garden, south-facing. I felt we could probably make quite a feature out of the garden, because a garden of that size is unusual in this area. Her husband had planted a lot of shrubs over the years, some fruit trees – mostly plums – and vines. There were vines trained against the walls, a vine along the wire fence, and at the bottom of the garden he'd put up two monstrous wooden greenhouses full of vines. He hadn't been able to prune these apparently for the past few years and so they were starting to crack the glass. She took me round showing me all the different varieties he'd planted. It seemed he'd bought a new variety every few years, hoping it would fruit, but none of them had. He'd wanted to make wine. All the equipment for making it was kept in a lean-to he'd built against the kitchen wall. The glass jars were muddled up with his tools, and – what's that powder – derris dust.

(*Amused:*) When I told her what price I felt we should put it on at, she said she thought it sounded rather high, and she'd have to think about it.

JAMES. A bargain.

CLAIR. Yes, but it's on the railway.

JAMES. Do you know what turmeric is?

CLAIR. You put it in curry. It makes it yellow.

JAMES. That's right.

CLAIR. When I left, there was a man looking at me out of the bedroom window.

JAMES. One of her children.

CLAIR. Because I'd been in all the rooms. They were all empty.

JAMES. I'll need to come along there.

CLAIR *kneels and begins picking up the cards.*

CLAIR. How was Rome?

JAMES. How was Rome?

Look, you shouldn't be doing that. Hot. Rome was hot.

CLAIR. And you exchange tomorrow.

JAMES. Tomorrow morning.

CLAIR *finishes clearing up the cards.* JAMES *stops measuring and watches.* CLAIR *senses his look and turns.*

JAMES. You shouldn't've done that.

CLAIR *moves out of the way. He measures.*

CLAIR. Your wife must be excited.

JAMES. Must she?

CLAIR. I thought you said you'd told her.

JAMES. Yes I did. Yes I have. And yes you're right she *is*. And of course the boy. Because it's a miserable life for Mark in that hotel. (CLAIR *looks at him.*) It's not good for a boy, is it. Do you have children?

CLAIR. No.

JAMES. I've asked you that before. And you gave me the same answer. You have no children. You live on your own. You're very happy on your own. I'm sorry. Because I think it's a kind of measure, isn't it, of people. There's a way of measuring people by listening to how often they repeat themselves. With some it's just the same thing every day. But with others – drunks for example, the insane – it's the same every moment of every day. And here am I repeating myself. Because it's funny isn't it, how you are terribly aware of everybody else's faults, and then you find you share them too.

CLAIR (*with a laugh*). Speak for yourself. (JAMES *also laughs. He folds up the rule.*) Well?

JAMES. What's that?

CLAIR. Will they fit?

JAMES. Do you know I'm hopeless at this sort of thing. What do *you* think? (*Both laugh.*)

CLAIR. Look, really we ought to go.

JAMES. But you're at lunch.

CLAIR *is holding the cards, flicking through them with her thumb.*

JAMES. Do you know, I think we're going to be very happy here. Since this will be our smallest house, but our biggest city. And I think there's a lot of nonsense spoken about cities, don't you. Because yes yes yes, we all know that strangers live next door to strangers. We've all passed friends in the street because the moment of recognition has occurred too late, and you're both too embarrassed – or something else – too. . . fixed, too fixed in your mind to turn. And yes yes yes, we've all, as strangers, woken up in the morning to find our faces inches away from the open eyes of another stranger. We get up. We dress on opposite sides of the bed. Then we fold the bed away maybe . . . A little ashamed perhaps, or at any rate too preoccupied to speak. But what does any of that matter? Because surely the great advantage is, that since we don't know each other, since we've never seen into each other's hearts, then we respect each other.

CLAIR. That would be nice if it was true.

JAMES. Isn't it true?

CLAIR *faint laugh.*

JAMES. Do you think it's the soil?

CLAIR. I'm sorry?

JAMES. May I have those? (*He takes the cards from* CLAIR.) The vines. Do you think perhaps it's the soil? (*He cuts the cards.*)

CLAIR. I'm not a gardener. (JAMES *gives her half the cards.*)

JAMES. Beggar my neighbour. What do you say.

CLAIR (*laughs*). Please . . .

JAMES. Well what then?

CLAIR. Look, I don't play cards.

JAMES. You don't play cards? Is this a matter of principle with you?

CLAIR (*laughs*). No . . .

JAMES. So what about snap then? You're not going to make a moral issue out of snap, are you. Money's not involved after all. Only chance. (*He sits.*) Yes yes yes, you have to go. Listen, one or two minutes, that's all.

A moment passes. CLAIR *sits to play.*

JAMES. Well there you are.

CLAIR. I should be at lunch.

JAMES. Well you are at lunch. This *is* lunch. Please.

CLAIR *lays the first card. Laying of cards gradually accelerates.*

JAMES (*with loud enthusiasm*). Snap!

He takes his cards. They lay cards as before.

Snap!

He takes his cards. They lay cards as before until JAMES *indicates to* CLAIR *to stop.*

Well?

CLAIR *faint laugh.*

JAMES. These two cards, aren't they the same?

CLAIR. Yes.

JAMES. Well.

,

You don't seem to be entering into the spirit.

,

Look, I'm giving you a chance, Clair. I wouldn't give everybody this kind of chance.

CLAIR *faint laugh.*

JAMES. Well? What is it you have to say?

CLAIR. Look, I . . . (*She gets up.*)

JAMES. Please, you have to say it.

CLAIR. I'm sorry, but this is ri –

JAMES. No it's not. I've said it. You must say it.

,

CLAIR. Snap.

JAMES. What?

CLAIR. Snap.

JAMES (*loud*). What? Snap?

CLAIR. Yes.

JAMES. Yes, well say it.

CLAIR (*loud*). Snap. (*Laughs.*)

JAMES (*gets up and gives her the cards*). These are yours. No. All of them. Please. They're all yours. You've won.

She takes the cards.

CLAIR. We ought to go.

JAMES. So what are you doing about eating?

CLAIR. I've got sandwiches.

JAMES. Well, another time.

CLAIR. Yes.

JAMES. What? (*Loud.*) What?

CLAIR (*loud*). Yes. (*Both laugh.*)

JAMES. Good.

But we won't will we.

CLAIR. I shouldn't think so.

JAMES. No. I shouldn't think so either.

Sound of laughter off.

Is there somebody here?

They listen. Silence. CLAIR moves to the hall doorway.

CLAIR (*calls*). Hello. (*Louder:*) Hello. (*Silence.*) There shouldn't be. (*She comes back to JAMES.*)

JAMES. It strikes me we're rather similar people, aren't we. I mean what is it, is there something wrong with us perhaps, that's what I'm beginning to wonder. Because here we are, we've been together in this room, this house, twice now. And –

CLAIR. Three times.

JAMES. Is it?

Do you know what I'd very much like to do now, Clair.

CLAIR *is about to speak but breaks off as she notices* JAMES' gaze shift *to a point behind her. She turns to see* ANNA *standing in the hall doorway.*

CLAIR. Oh. Hello. I'm sorry about this.

ANNA. It's my day off.

CLAIR. Yes, I'm sorry. I was told there'd be no one here.

ANNA. This is my day off.

CLAIR. Yes of course. (*To* JAMES:) They told me the house would be empty.

VITTORIO, *a young man smoking a cigarette, comes in behind* ANNA *and puts his arms around her waist. She puts her hands on his.*

CLAIR. Anyway. Listen. I think we've – haven't we – finished – is that right?

ANNA. Please don't tell Mrs Walsum.

CLAIR (*to* JAMES). You didn't want to look upstairs. Did you?

VITTORIO (*sotto voce*). Non è la loro, vero?

ANNA (*sotto voce*). No, lei è l'agente immobiliare.

VITTORIO. Cosa? Ha la chiave?

ANNA. Non ha importanza.

ANNA *takes the cigarette and inhales before returning it to* VITTORIO'*s hand. Neither of them shows any embarrassment.*

CLAIR. Listen, I'm sorry if we've . . . Look, I was told there'd be no one here.

ANNA. Please don't tell them, OK.

VITTORIO. Guarderanno di sopra?

ANNA. No. Se ne andranno.

VITTORIO. Ma tu passerai dei guai.

ANNA. No. Non lo diranno a nessuno.

JAMES. Well of course we won't. Of course we won't tell anyone.

ANNA. Thank you.

VITTORIO *and* ANNA *go.*

JAMES. Do you know what I'd very much like to do now, Clair. I'd like to go out into the garden.

Blackout.

3

Afternoon. LIZ *and* MIKE. *Both quiet and tense.*

MIKE. Well he might show. I suppose he might still show.

LIZ. Yes.

MIKE. I mean what are they doing, are they phoning?

LIZ. They've been phoning.

MIKE. Well are they sending someone?

LIZ. I don't know.

MIKE. Well you've spoken to them.

LIZ. I told you I don't know.

,

MIKE. I'm sorry.

,

LIZ. I mean –   ⎫
                       ⎬ (*together*)
MIKE. But listen –   ⎭

,

Well come on.

LIZ. Nothing.

MIKE. You were going to say something.

LIZ. It's nothing.

,

All I was going to say was –

MIKE. I mean since you interrupted me.

LIZ. Well go on then.

MIKE. No no. Please. You were going to say something.

,

LIZ. All I was going to say was is it's obvious he's not going to.

MIKE. Is that what they said?

LIZ. No, but it's obvious.

MIKE. I don't see that it's obvious.

LIZ. You know it's obvious.

,

Look, we both know it's obvious.

MIKE. But he must have a number, he must have an address.

LIZ. Yes.

MIKE. Well are they sending someone?

LIZ. Well obviously not.

MIKE. Is that what they said?

LIZ. Look, I can't repeat . . .

MIKE. I know you can't.

LIZ. . . . word for word what they said.

MIKE. I know you can't, but they must've said something.

LIZ. I've told you what they said.

MIKE. Well it keeps changing.

LIZ. It doesn't keep changing. They appreciate our position but there's nothing they can do.

MIKE. Well I'm sorry but I find that hard to believe.

LIZ. Well you speak to them.

MIKE. I'm not speaking to them.

,

All I want to know is what's happening.

LIZ. We know what's happened.

MIKE. We don't know what's happened. What's happened is everyone thinks they know what's happened.

LIZ. Well it's obvious what's happened.

MIKE. Well I don't see that it's obvious.

,

Well I'm sorry, and perhaps there's something wrong with me but I don't see that it's at all obvious, because the fact remains –

LIZ. Well look, if you refuse to see it –

MIKE. The fact remains that what we're talking about here are two quite unrelated things.

LIZ. Well of course they're related.

MIKE. Yes, that's the assumption.

LIZ. Well if you refuse to be realistic about it.

MIKE. I'm sorry, I'm sorry, but look what is this? What is this? Because what I'm trying to be *is* realistic, that's exactly my point. Because everyone else is just letting their imagina –

LIZ. Well listen, you talk to them.

MIKE. I'm not talking to them.

LIZ. Well if you won't talk to them.

,

MIKE. Because the fact remains –

LIZ. I mean if you won't even talk to them.

MIKE. The fact remains, doesn't it, that we know her movements and we know she went back to work in the afternoon.

LIZ. No.

,

No she didn't.

MIKE. You said she did.

LIZ. I've already told you she didn't.

MIKE. You said she didn't go in this morning.

LIZ. I said – if you'd listened you would've heard that what I said

was was she hasn't been in this morning and she didn't go back
yesterday afternoon.

MIKE. Well if you'd told me that.

LIZ. I have told you that.

MIKE. I mean if you'd just told me that in the first place.

                                    ,

It's all we need, isn't it.

LIZ. Mike.

MIKE. I just mean this is all we need.

LIZ. Yes but there is Clair, there is Clair to consider.

MIKE. Well fuck quite frankly, fuck Clair.
No, look, I'm sorry, I'm sorry. Because if that's what's happened
although I still don't really see that it's likely then naturally,
naturally I have every sympathy for Clair. But Jesus Christ the fact
remains the man was supposed to exchange. Because couldn't
he've waited? Yes yes yes I know it's terrible.

                                    ,

I mean obviously . . .

                                    ,

Fuck.

                                    ,

Look, you know I like Clair. I've always said: I like Clair.

LIZ. Yes I know.

MIKE. Well what's that supposed to mean?

                                    ,

I mean what is that supposed to mean exactly?

LIZ. I just mean if you'd gone round with him instead . . .

MIKE. That's Clair's job. Clair is paid – she is paid – by us –
whatever per cent – to go round with people. Because –

LIZ. All right, I know.

MIKE. Well come on.

                                    ,

I mean if she can't look after herself.

,

Because listen, let's be realistic about this. What are we supposed to imagine? Are we supposed to imagine he took her by the throat and dragged her off . . .

LIZ. No obviously not.

MIKE. Dragged her off in broad daylight – this was what, lunchtime – to his . . . whatever it was.

,

LIZ. BMW.

MIKE. BMW.

Both faint laugh. They relax a little.

MIKE. Because –

LIZ. No, obviously it wasn't like that.

MIKE. Well then.

,

And you say Anna was here.

LIZ. That's right.

MIKE. And she witnessed this . . . I don't know . . . rape, abduction, or whatever.

LIZ (*on the word 'rape'*). Well obviously it's more complicated than that.

MIKE. Because isn't it rather condescending to assume that Clair is a victim in this? Because given the choice, who's to say she'd not rather go somewhere, do something, go somewhere interesting, rather than trot off back to work and sell houses.

LIZ. The French Pyrenees.

MIKE. What?

,

LIZ. Look, let's not argue about it.

MIKE. So what was Anna doing here anyway?

LIZ. I've no idea.

MIKE. Well surely you asked.

LIZ. I haven't had time.

MIKE. But you've spoken to her. Because she was meant to be out all day.

LIZ. Yes I know she was.

MIKE. So what was she doing in the house?

LIZ. Well how do I know what she was doing in the house?

MIKE. We ought to talk to her.

LIZ. Well you talk to her.

MIKE. I'm not talking to her.

The baby is crying.

Fuck.

LIZ. Mmm?

MIKE. She's awake.

,

Anyway what did they have to say?

LIZ. Well they were apologetic.

MIKE. You mentioned the Harraps. (*i.e. to the agent.*)

LIZ. No, we've lost the Harraps.

MIKE. You're sure.

LIZ. They're building a complex. They've got permission to build one of these . . . a timeshare complex on the land.

MIKE. But it's protected.

LIZ. Obviously not.

,

MIKE. So they're laughing.

The crying has grown louder.

Jesus Christ.

LIZ (*goes to doorway*). Anna. (*Louder:*) Anna. The thing was (*Faint laugh.*) well I don't know but I felt he was implying –

MIKE. Which one is that?

LIZ. It was Toby.

MIKE. What, at the back?

LIZ. No, he's on the right as you go in. No, I felt that he –

MIKE. Toby.

LIZ. Yes, was implying that we could, well I'm fairly sure this is what he was trying to say . . .

MIKE. Wait a moment. (*Goes to doorway and calls:*) Anna. She's awake. (*He's about to go out when the crying stops. Silence.*) How d'you mean?

LIZ. Well I just felt he had an idea we could, well exploit the situation.

MIKE. Exploit it.

LIZ. I think so.

MIKE. Well is that what he said?

LIZ. No it's not what he *said*.

,

All I mean is is he was talking about perhaps – because of course I agreed they should leave it on – so he just felt that perhaps it could be a good opportunity to . . . reconsider I suppose.

MIKE. What, the price?

LIZ. The price, because apparently there's been a lot of . . . activity over the past few weeks, and I think he was implying that Clair, well, had perhaps been a little too cautious.

,

He felt for example she hadn't been making enough of the fourth bedroom.

,

MIKE. Well this is assuming we've lost James.

,

LIZ. Well I think we have to assume we've lost James.

,

MIKE. So he thinks two hundred is cautious.

,

LIZ. That's basically what he's saying.

MIKE. Well of course that's what we've always said ourselves.

LIZ. Well that's right.

MIKE *moves away, laughs briefly, reflects.*

LIZ. I mean this was all very informal because I don't want to give the wrong impression, because actually he was very upset about Clair.

LIZ *comes up behind* MIKE *and puts her arms around his waist. He puts his hands on hers.*

MIKE. What is it?

LIZ. Aren't you curious?

,

It's just they've been here, haven't they. They were in this house.

They were in this room, that's all.

,

I mean aren't you curious?

MIKE. Mmm?

LIZ. Because in some ways I can't imagine it at all, I can't imagine where they'd begin.

,

But then I suppose they're rather similar people.

MIKE. D'you think?

,

LIZ. No, don't let go. Don't let go of me.

,

MIKE. Anna might come in.

LIZ. Well let her come in.

Blackout.

4

We hear JAMES *speaking in the darkness. Then the lights come up faintly on* CLAIR's *flat at night, as before.* JAMES *talks softly on the phone, very much at his ease, wearing a pair of white gloves. Beside him on the unmade bed, not immediately noticeable, is a bag.*

JAMES (*ad lib*). Yes . . . yes . . . well yes . . . yes of course you do.

The lights come up.

Yes. I know. (*Faint laugh.*) I do understand.

No, I think that's very sensible of you. Because I'd probably do exactly the same thing in your shoes. (*Confidential:*) To tell you the truth I'm a bit of a worrier myself.

Two of a kind. (*Laughs.*) Yes, maybe we are (*Laughs.*) Yes, I like that.

He reaches for the bag which we recognise from the previous scenes as CLAIR's.

Oh yes. Very old friends.

Silence. He contemplates the bag. The sound of a train approaching.

Hello. – Yes. Sorry. I was dreaming.

Clair? – No, I'm afraid she's not here. – I said I'm afraid she's not here.

A high-speed train passes in the middle-distance, projecting shadows across the room. As it does so, JAMES *empties the contents of* CLAIR's *bag out onto the bed, or onto a bedside table. These include various keys with numbered tags, a pack of sandwiches, and some papers – details of houses – which slip down onto the floor.* JAMES *picks absently through these objects as he speaks, perhaps lining the keys up a row.*

Yes I'm sorry, I didn't catch that. There was a train.

That's right, I'm afraid she's not back. Was she expecting you to call? These trains are a nuisance, aren't they.

No, I'm afraid I don't know her movements at all. Presumably she's working late. Now would you believe there's another one coming.

As the train passes, JAMES *turns to the window and watches it. The train recedes. Silence.*

Yes, hello . . . – (*Faint laugh.*) Dreaming again. I do apologise. Railway tracks are such a model of perspective, aren't they. The sleepers bunch up as the lines converge on the vanishing point.

Well yes I think it's fair to assume she's at work, don't you.
Because as you probably know they're open in the evenings now.

As he sorts through the things he comes across a photograph.

You're right, it's a hateful business. And of course she's caught in
the middle of it. But then it's better than waitressing, wouldn't
you say. – (*Laughs.*)

You're joking. I deal in pictures. – I said I deal in pictures, not
houses. – Well I enjoy it.

Well yes, but you have to remember her prospects are much
better in the city. Because, and of course I entirely respect your
opinion which is a perfectly tenable one, but I do sometimes
think there's a lot of nonsense spoken about cities, I'm afraid.
The fear. The loneliness. – Yes, because it needn't be like that,
and quite frankly too much intimacy can be just as stifling. I
mean I've always found it easier to get on, in a way, among
strangers. – Yes, because you can take more risks.

Oh no no no. Of course she wouldn't take any risks. – No, not in
the way you mean. It was merely a figure of speech. No if
anything I'd say she was cautious.

Yes I know, (*Confidential:*) But to be honest I think she's much
happier being on her own. I think it's important to respect that. –
Pretty well. – Oh yes, very old friends.

Do I have what? – No, please, you're not prying at all. Yes I do
have a key as a matter of fact. It's just an arrangement we have. –
That's right, a useful arrangement.

Haven't you? Well that's a shame. But perhaps she feels there
wouldn't be room to have you stay. Because it is rather small.
When I first saw it I must admit I thought I'd stumbled into a
large cupboard. – (*Laughs.*) Yes. I did. But then you see with the
prices here being what they are. – Exactly. Just spiralling. And of
course *I* was probably just the same with *my* mother. Because you
do value your independence at that age. I don't think you should
take it too seriously. Because after all, and this isn't to belittle
her, she's still only a girl.

(*Thinking aloud as he looks as the photograph:*) This is you, isn't it.

(*Faint laugh.*) Nothing. No, it's nothing. (*He lays the picture
carefully down.*) Of course what she really needs, what she actually
needs, is one of those sofas isn't it, that turns into a bed. It may

be small but I'd say there was certainly room for one of those sofas that turns into a bed, wouldn't you. – Can't you? Now I'm quite the opposite, because I can sleep anywhere, trains, anywhere. In fact I often say I'd rather sleep on a train than in a proper bed, given the choice. – I think it's the movement. There's something very soothing about constant movement, isn't there. And waking up in a totally different place. That's always been a passion of mine, waking up in a totally different place.

You're right, it does take all sorts, doesn't it. (*Faint laugh.*)

Is she? – Well no she didn't tell me that. But of course I'm sure she'll sell it very easily. – That depends what you mean by desirable. It faces north, but then for some people, artists and so on, that kind of light is an advantage. – Oh yes. Because it's so even, and white.

Really? Bank Holiday Monday?

(*He looks around.*) Yes, very nicely. That's right, mostly peach. – Yes, I like peach. Because you can put almost anything with it, can't you. – Warmth. Exactly.

He takes the pack of sandwiches, opens it with his teeth, and shakes the sandwiches out during the following.

Yes.

Yes, you're quite right. She *has*.

Yes, I know.

Yes, I think she *does*, doesn't she.

Well I'm glad you feel happier there's a man here, and I quite understand how you must worry, particularly in the present climate. Because there always seems to be a question mark over one's security these days, doesn't there. But listen, I really don't want to disparage this room. On the contrary, there's a good atmosphere here. A sense of sanctuary. And that's what matters after all. Between trains at least, you can make yourself at home. It feels very much like home. Particularly the silence. – The silence, because I do appreciate silence.

He picks up a sandwich and parts the bread to examine the filling.

Well actually I'm thinking of eating.

Oh no, please, I'm not in the middle of anything. I'm just thinking about it. Because I've got a sandwich here and it's just occurred to me do you know I don't think I've eaten all day.

Well that's what I'm trying to work out as a matter of fact. I've a suspicion it's egg. – Yes, I like egg. But the bread is white, and I try to stick to brown whenever I can.

Do you? Because these were all I could get hold of.

Do you? Well I think opinion is divided, isn't it.

You're quite right, it *is* a dilemma. I think we're plagued these days, aren't we, by dilemmas. – (*Laugh.*) – (*Bigger laugh.*) I couldn't agree more.

Well listen, I'm glad I've spoken to *you*. Because I'll admit I was in two minds about answering the phone here. Do you know what I mean? But the thing is, is there's nothing worse is there than watching a telephone ring, just watching it ring. There's nothing more desolate really. – Desolate, nothing more lonely. And I'm afraid I do like talking. It's important to be aware of your faults isn't it, and mine I know is a passion, a terrible passion for the sound of my own voice. – No, really it is, I could easily go on like this all night.

(*Laughs.*) Well yes I know. It does soon mount up. But then what's money.

Well. Yes. – (*Laughs.*) Yes. Listen – (*He's interrupted.*)

He sorts through the objects from CLAIR*'s bag. He finds the playing cards in a packet. He shakes them out during the following.*

Sorry? – Yes, I would.

Yes, why not wait now till tomorrow, because, well, what is the time now? – It's not, is it? Do you know I had no idea.

Well of course I will.

Your love. Yes of course I will. You are . . .?

Yes, of course you are. I'm sorry, we've already established that. Because you have the same eyes.

What did I say? Did I say eyes? – No, I mean voice. You have the same voice. Did I say eyes? Do you know I think I must be tired. – Yes, I'm beginning to feel a little tired. The fact is I've not eaten all day.

He begins setting the cards out very slowly face up in rows.

Yes, but the question is, can I really face egg? Can I really face egg, or what looks like egg, in white bread? You know, I don't think I can. Because I say I've not eaten, but really I've no appetite either. That's the truth of the matter. No appetite. – (*Laughs.*) You could well be right.

He continues to make rows of cards.

Well of course I will.

Your love, yes I'll make a note of it.

No, I don't think I can wait. Because I've feeling she'll be late. I've a feeling she'll be very late, actually. – Oh, it's just a feeling.

No, I don't think I can. I'd like to. Because of course we were supposed to be having lunch together as a matter of fact. That's why I'm here as a matter of fact. But it looks like lunch is off.

What did I say? Did I say lunch? – No, I mean dinner. Because I say I've no appetite but of course we were supposed to be having dinner together. What, did I say lunch?

Yes, it is a pity. But the thing is is I have to be in Rome in the morning. – That's right. Rome.

No, it's business. – Oh, I travel a lot on business. And the thing is is you can see from the slides it's not genuine.

Well I'm afraid like all these things the attribution is what determines the value.

(*Faint laugh.*) Yes, but the heat makes me rather irritable. Whenever I go a long way south I tend to languish rather, don't you? – I said I tend to languish, don't you?

Haven't you? Well you should go. You could see a lot in seven days.

Couldn't you manage that? Well a long weekend then. Why not try a long weekend. – That's right, talk to him about it.

Yes, goodnight then.

Of course I will. I've made a note of it.

Goodnight. – Not at all. – Not at all. It's been a pleasure.

He breaks off the call. The sound of a train approaching.

Goodnight.

He replaces the receiver. As he continues to set out the cards, the train passes, closer and louder than the previous trains, projecting shadows across the room. The light fades with the sound of the receding train.

5

MIKE *and LIZ's garden. October evening sunlight.* MIKE, LIZ *and* TOBY. MIKE *and* LIZ *are drinking wine. As the lights come up, the three of them are laughing.* ANNA *sits by the vine, reading a book.*

MIKE. You're joking . . .

TOBY. I am not. I swear to you those were her exact words.

MIKE. Consider an offer . . .

TOBY. That's right. "I'm prepared to consider an offer."

LIZ. But you must've *died* . . .

TOBY. And the thing is, is there she is – I mean it wouldn't've been so bad – but there she is standing at the top of the stairs, and all she's got on – well as far as I could tell (*Laughs.*) – all she's wearing is this, well a kind of Chinese dressing-gown, one of these . . . kimonos.

MIKE. Japanese, in that case.

TOBY. Well whatever it was I couldn't get out of there fast enough,

They all three laugh a little more. Silence.

MIKE. Yes, Anna's got one of those, hasn't she.

LIZ. One of what?

MIKE. One of those – whatever it is – kimonos.

LIZ. Has she?

MIKE. You know she has.

It's got birds on it.

TOBY. It's certainly very pleasant out here.

LIZ. Well it's quiet at least.

MIKE. The thing is we're not really gardeners.

TOBY. Well you wouldn't believe it.

LIZ. Because of course we used to get a lot of noise from next door, when it was flats.

MIKE. Well of course it still is flats.

LIZ. Yes, but when it was tenants.

TOBY *nods in sympathy.*

MIKE. Mind you, when you think about it, there's absolutely no reason why a tenant – is there – should make any more noise than an owner-occupier.

TOBY. No, but I'm afraid – let's face it – I'm afraid you're talking about a completely different sort of person, a completely different sort of attitude to the property.

LIZ. Of course it's quite disgusting what they did to the tenants.

MIKE. Well it's unforgiveable.

LIZ. The nice thing is, by this time of day the light's come round.

TOBY *glances at his watch.*

LIZ. Look, I'm sorry, can we get you a glass of wine?

TOBY. I'd rather not, actually.

MIKE. No no. Fine. We understand. Because obviously you must still feel – well of course it's not as if we don't still feel –

LIZ. Yes, but life has to go on, Mike.

MIKE. Well of course life has to go on. By definition life has to go on. It's just –

TOBY. Please. It's just a little early for me, that's all. (*Faint laugh.*) But I wouldn't say no to something soft.

LIZ. What, squash?

TOBY. Fine. Yes. Squash.

MIKE. Or a Coke or something?

TOBY. Squash would be fine.

LIZ. Anna, could you be a darling and get a glass of squash for Mr –

TOBY. Toby. Please, it's Toby.

LIZ. Right. Yes, of course. Could you get him a glass of orange squash.

ANNA. Orange squash.

TOBY. Or lemon. Lemon would be fine.

ANNA *doesn't move.*

LIZ. You'd like some ice in it.

TOBY. Please. (*To* ANNA:) Yes please, lots of ice.

ANNA *nods, but has not understood.*

LIZ. Squash, Anna.

ANNA. Squash.

TOBY. Well anything really. Anything soft.

LIZ. Look, I'd better go with her. I won't be a moment.

LIZ *and* ANNA *go off.* TOBY *involuntarily turns to watch* ANNA *go.*

MIKE. It's our perennial problem.

TOBY (*turns back*). I'm sorry?

MIKE. Getting her dressed.

TOBY. Right.

MIKE. I mean getting her to get dressed. Not actually . . . dressing her.

TOBY (*nods*). Right right. (*He takes out cigarettes.*)

I suppose she's in the bath a lot, or something.

MIKE. Because our major fear was naturally that her appearance would, well put people off.

TOBY. Yes?

MIKE. Only in that, she possibly creates the impression –

TOBY (*lights up*). Well she wouldn't put me off quite frankly.

TOBY *laughs.* MIKE *joins in. Brief laugh together.*

MIKE. Listen, really we just wanted to thank you for everything you've done, and –

LIZ (*coming out*). There's only lemon I'm afraid.

TOBY. No, that's fine.

LIZ (*calls*). No, lemon's fine, Anna. It's surprising really just how limited her vocabulary actually is.

TOBY. She's French is she?

MIKE. Italian actually. Naples.

LIZ. It's the phone bills we dread.

TOBY. Well as long as it's not Australia.

All faint laugh.

LIZ. Look, the thing is, is we just wanted to thank you for everything you've done, and – (ANNA *enters with squash.*) That's right, if you could just give it to Mr –

TOBY. Toby.

LIZ. I'm sorry. To Toby. (ANNA *gives him the drink.*)

TOBY. Thanks. (ANNA *returns to her book.*)

LIZ. Well. Cheers.

TOBY. Cheers.

MIKE. Cheers.

LIZ (*sotto voce*). Has she just had another bath?

MIKE (*sotto voce*). I've really no idea what she's been doing.

LIZ (*to* TOBY). You can't imagine the trouble we've had getting her dressed.

TOBY. No, your husband was . . .

LIZ. I mean with people coming round to view all the time.

MIKE (*jovial*). Well getting her to get dressed. Not actually getting her dressed.

LIZ. Well obviously not getting her dressed, Mike.

Obviously she can dress herself.

MIKE. Look, is that cold enough for you?

TOBY. I'm sorry?

MIKE. No, sorry, I just thought for a moment there was no ice in it.

TOBY *swirls the drink. The ice clinks.*

MIKE. Anyway, as Liz was saying, we just wanted to thank you for everything you've done, and . . . Well obviously we're delighted.

LIZ (*laughs*). I mean the price was . . .

MIKE (*laughs*). Well actually when you think about it it's quite ridiculous . . .

LIZ. Well the whole thing's ridiculous . . .

MIKE. It just stops meaning anything after a while . . .

LIZ. Because we'll be honest, we thought two hundred was probably pushing it, didn't we.

MIKE. The absurd thing is that we would almost certainly 've taken less. Well particularly after . . .

LIZ. But two hundred and fifty . . .

MIKE. I know. It's crazy.

LIZ. It's quite crazy.

MIKE. I mean talk about spiralling . . . Two hundred and fifty. And cash.

LIZ. Well yes that's the amazing thing: cash.

MIKE *and* LIZ *both chuckle.* TOBY *looks on, swirling the ice in his glass.*

TOBY. Yes, I feel we've achieved quite a favourable price. Although maybe not so remarkable for four bedrooms in the present climate. Of course the Baldwins had been recently disappointed by some vendors who had behaved – how shall we say? – rather less than honourably. (*All faint laugh.*) So naturally the fact that you could offer them early possession was a strong point in your favour.

So . . . what exactly is your position now?

LIZ. Well naturally we're looking.

TOBY. And of course you are yourselves cash. Right. And your price?

LIZ. Well round about three hundred, isn't it.

MIKE. Well let's say we could be talking about three fifty for something exceptional.

TOBY. Three hundred and fifty. Right.

LIZ. The thing is, is we feel it's important to take our time.

TOBY. No, I understand that.

MIKE (*laughs*). It's just some friends of ours . . .

LIZ (*laughs*). Poor Poppy and Max . . .

MIKE. They panicked completely and ended up living on a railway.

They all laugh.

MIKE. Mind you. It's quite a place. They've put in marble floors. Three bathrooms.

LIZ. Yes, but the trains . . . They're horribly overlooked, Mike.

TOBY *glances at his watch.* MIKE *takes the bottle.*

MIKE. Listen, you're sure you won't . . .

TOBY *covers his glass with his hand like* ANNA *at the end of Act One, Scene One. Silence.* MIKE *pours more wine for himself and* LIZ.

LIZ (*laughs*). I think the thing is – isn't it – is that in a ridiculous kind of way we feel, well responsible.

MIKE (*laughs*). Well responsible probably isn't the right word.

LIZ. No no, obviously not *responsible*.

MIKE. Because I think it would be wrong, I've said to Liz I think it would actually be morally wrong, for any of us to feel responsible, in that way.

LIZ. Well no, I don't mean responsible.

MIKE. Well you said responsible.

LIZ. Yes I know that's what I *said*, Mike.

TOBY *swirls his ice. He's looking at* ANNA.

MIKE (*to* TOBY, *with a note of aggression*). I mean, what do you feel?

TOBY (*turns back*). I'm sorry? (*Looks at watch.*) Look, actually I ought to be . . .

MIKE. I mean my wife seems to feel we are, in some obscure way, responsible. So I just wondered –

LIZ. Please Mike.

MIKE. Look I just want to know what the man thinks for godsake.

,

TOBY. Well . . . (*Faint laugh.*) Surely if they . . . knew, if they knew about the railway when they bought it . . . then surely . . .

MIKE. The railway.

TOBY. Yes, if they knew about it when they bought it, then surely . . . unless there are . . . factors I don't know about. Then surely

... well they can hardly hold either of you responsible for the purchase. (*Laughs.*) Can they?

MIKE. No no. You're quite right.

TOBY. Look, I'm afraid I have to –

MIKE. Go. Yes. Of course.

TOBY. It's just I've . . .

MIKE. Of course. No. We understand.

TOBY. I'm meant to be – very boring – meeting some people for a meal that's all.

LIZ. Well we're very grateful to you for dropping by.

MIKE. Yes. Thanks again.

TOBY *shakes hands with* MIKE *and* LIZ.

TOBY. I'll see myself out.

LIZ. No. Please . . . (LIZ *makes to go with* TOBY.)

MIKE. The key.

They turn back.

TOBY. I'm sorry?

LIZ. Yes of course. Now it's all over – thankgod – we meant to ask you for our key.

TOBY. The key.

MIKE. Well it doesn't have to be now. Whenever you can . . .

TOBY. No. Look. Sorry. I thought you'd . . . Because the thing is of course Clair had your key.

MIKE. Clair. Right. No. (*Faint laugh.*) Look, sorry.

TOBY. No no. Our fault entirely.

LIZ. Well it's hardly . . .

TOBY. No no. Obviously you must feel – well I think anybody would feel – because you're not the only people in this position, obviously. But yes I quite understand that you must feel there's a . . . question mark, if you like, over your security. Naturally the best thing would be to change the locks, but as you're moving out in a few days . . . Look. No problem. I'll speak to the Baldwins about it.

MIKE. But I'm sure it's — ⎫
⎬ (*together*)
LIZ. Please — ⎭

TOBY. No. Really. It's no trouble. I'll speak to them in the morning. (*About to go, with a nervous gesture to the garden.*) They loved the vine.

Blackout.